NATIONAL
GEOGRAPHIC
KiDS

weird
but
true! 9

NATIONAL GEOGRAPHIC KiDS

weird but true! 9

300 outrageous facts

NATIONAL GEOGRAPHIC
WASHINGTON, D.C.

The planet **Venus** may have once been **habitable.**

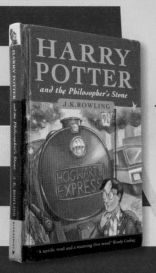

Some **500** first-edition copies of *Harry Potter and the Philosopher's Stone* were printed with a **typo**—and are now worth tens of thousands of dollars.

A SCIENTIST IN MEXICO HAS **DEVELOPED THE TECHNOLOGY TO CREATE GLOW-IN-THE-DARK SIDEWALKS.**

AN ARTIST USED **NESTS** FROM **WASPS AND HORNETS** TO CREATE A HUMAN-SIZE SCULPTURE OF A QUEEN BEE.

Some types of **algae** eat themselves when food is scarce.

SOUTH AMERICAN **ANTS** HAVE BEEN **FARMING FUNGI** FOR 60 MILLION YEARS.

WHITE ADMIRAL BUTTERFLY POOP SMELLS LIKE MINT.

The second **new moon** in a **month** is called a **black moon.**

BLACK MOONS OCCUR ONLY ABOUT ONCE EVERY 32 MONTHS.

Some **mosquitoes** prefer **cow blood** to **human blood.**

A **spider** in Australia **breathes underwater** and eats **toads.**

GULP!

9

Scientists have figured out how to...

...turn rotten **tomatoes** into **energy.**

...turn rats **transparent.**

boo!

...turn plastic trash into **fuel.**

...make a substance similar to **kryptonite**.

...create a **battery** inspired by **vitamins**.

...make a toilet that can **generate electricity** from **urine**.

11

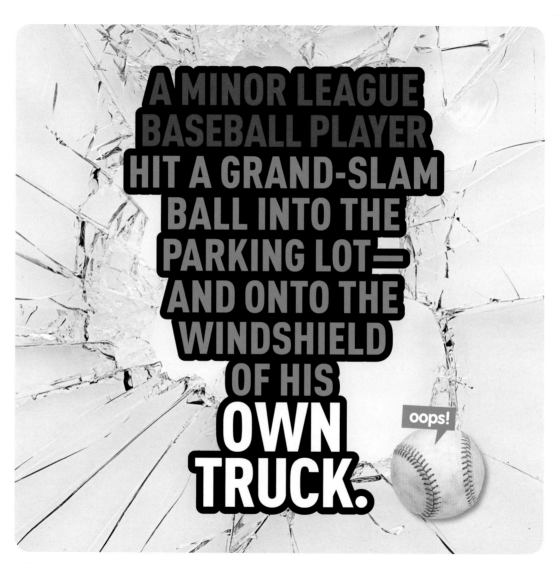

A MINOR LEAGUE BASEBALL PLAYER HIT A GRAND-SLAM BALL INTO THE PARKING LOT—AND ONTO THE WINDSHIELD OF HIS **OWN TRUCK.**

oops!

The **metal** in one of **King Tut's daggers** was made using **iron** from a **meteorite**.

A COMPANY IN SPAIN **DEVELOPED A 3-D PRINTER THAT CAN MAKE PIZZA.**

TWO TEENAGERS IN WISCONSIN, U.S.A., BUILT A BACKYARD **ROLLER COASTER.**

A **pair of birds** in Angus, Scotland, regularly **steal underwear and socks** from **swimmers.**

14

The world's first year-round ice hotel opened in Sweden.

There are
130 species of fish
that spend at least
some of their time
on dry land.

THE MANCHINEEL TREE IS SO **TOXIC** THAT EVEN STANDING UNDER IT IN RAINY WEATHER IS DANGEROUS.

OLYMPIC GOLD MEDALS ARE WORTH AROUND $600.

You can **swim** as fast in **syrup** as you can in **water.**

A GIANT INFLATABLE MOON ROLLED OVER TRAFFIC ON A BUSY HIGHWAY IN CHINA.

SCIENTISTS RECENTLY DISCOVERED A PREHISTORIC **SCORPION** THAT GREW AS LONG AS A HUMAN.

The **town** of Codell, Kansas, U.S.A., was hit by a **tornado** on **May 20** in **1916, 1917,** and **1918.**

Scientists put fitness-tracking technology on squirrels to see how much energy they used.

SOME FLOWER ARRANGEMENTS IN VICTORIAN ENGLAND CONTAINED CODED MESSAGES.

GORiLLAS SOMETIMES SING HAPPY SONGS WHEN THEY EAT.

22

A hotel straddling the border of France and Switzerland lets you sleep with your head in one country and your feet in the other.

THE U.S.-CANADIAN BORDER RUNS THROUGH THE MIDDLE OF A LIBRARY.

Some **scientists** think that most of the **universe** is trapped inside **ancient black holes.**

A **HUMAN** HAS ROUGHLY THE SAME NUMBER OF **GENES** AS A **MICROSCOPIC WORM.**

SCIENTISTS HAVE ENGINEERED **SPINACH** PLANTS THAT CAN **DETECT** BOMBS.

Every August, people in Bolivia gather to **break rocks** for **good luck.**

Sociable **weavers** build "apartment" nests that can house up to 500 birds.

THE COMMUNAL **NESTS** CAN **WEIGH** AS MUCH AS A SMALL **CAR.**

A BILLIONAIRE BOUGHT **EIGHT** **$1,000** SMARTPHONES— FOR HIS **DOG.**

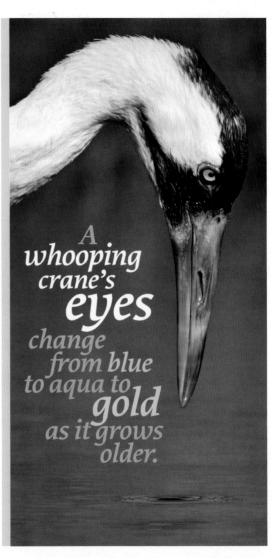

A *whooping crane's* *eyes* change *from blue to aqua to* **gold** *as it grows older.*

Thieves in Wisconsin, U.S.A., stole 20,000 pounds (9,072 kg) of cheese.

SCIENTISTS USED BACTERIA TO MAKE A MICROSCOPIC WIND FARM.

There are decomposed **wasps** inside of figs.

Flat millipedes shoot a defensive spray that smells like cherry cola.

33

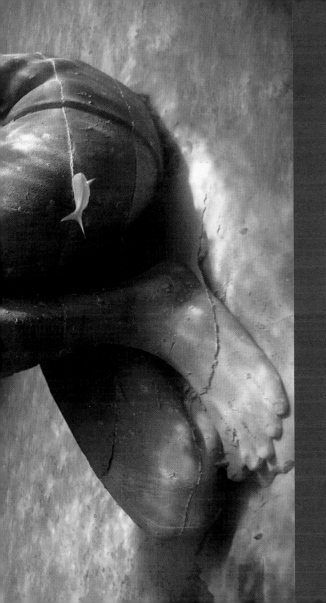

THERE'S A SCULPTURE AS TALL AS A GIRAFFE SITTING ON THE OCEAN FLOOR IN THE BAHAMAS.

MOTHS ARE EVOLVING TO BE LESS ATTRACTED TO LIGHT.

A **New York City museum** offered visitors the chance to use an **18-karat-gold toilet.**

A CITY IN GERMANY INSTALLED **TRAFFIC SIGNALS** ON ITS **SIDEWALKS.**

THE CONTINENT OF AUSTRALIA MOVES BACK AND FORTH WHEN THE SEASONS CHANGE.

AUSTRALIA HAS DRIFTED ALMOST FIVE FEET (1.5 m) NORTH IN THE PAST 22 YEARS.

IN TAIWAN, IT'S TRENDY TO GET YOUR DOG'S FUR GROOMED INTO GEOMETRIC SHAPES.

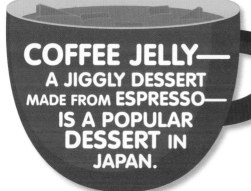

COFFEE JELLY— A JIGGLY DESSERT MADE FROM **ESPRESSO—** IS A POPULAR **DESSERT** IN JAPAN.

BLACK HOLES "EAT" STARS AND "BURP" GAS.

Researchers observed a **sea lion** named **Ronan** bobbing her head in time with **music.**

SOME BIRDS "TALK" TO THEIR UNHATCHED EGGS.
DOGS CAN UNDERSTAND HUMAN SPEECH.

Leonardo da Vinci may have written backward

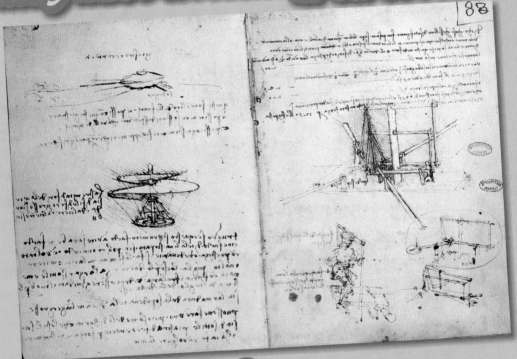

to keep people from stealing his ideas.

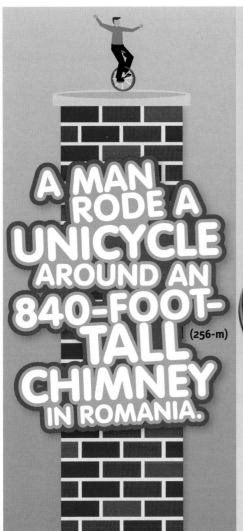

A MAN RODE A UNICYCLE AROUND AN 840-FOOT-TALL CHIMNEY IN ROMANIA.

(256-m)

Chork= chopsticks + fork

A man accidentally discovered a **49,000-year-old** human settlement while taking a **bathroom break** in an Australian park.

43

The pop-up **Museum** of **Ice Cream** in New York City featured a swimmable **pool** full of faux **rainbow sprinkles.**

 **DRAGONFLIES CAN LIVE UNDERWATER FOR TWO YEARS.**

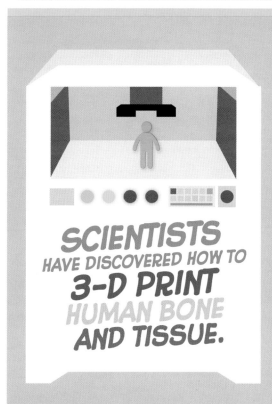

SCIENTISTS HAVE DISCOVERED HOW TO **3-D PRINT** HUMAN BONE AND TISSUE.

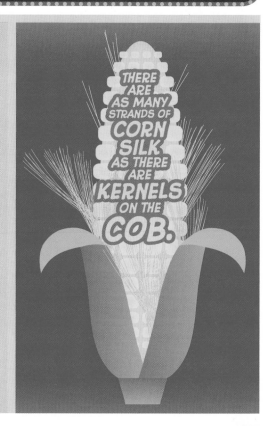

THERE ARE AS MANY STRANDS OF **CORN SILK** AS THERE ARE **KERNELS** ON THE **COB.**

A family in New Jersey, U.S.A., lives in a farmhouse encased in an aircraft hangar.

FRESHWATER
SNAILS **KILL**
MORE HUMANS
EVERY YEAR
THAN DO LIONS,
WOLVES, CROCODILES,
AND SHARKS
COMBINED.

Some
piranhas are
vegetarian.

THE LAWS OF **PHYSICS** DO NOT RULE OUT TIME TRAVEL.

You can buy a **smartphone case** that looks like an **ice-cream sandwich.**

Early **ketchup** recipes included mushrooms, oysters, and walnuts—but no tomatoes.

A NEW SPECIES OF **TROPICAL ANT** WAS RECENTLY **DISCOVERED IN A FROG'S BELLY.**

49

It costs the **U.S. Mint** about **eight cents** to make **one nickel.**

Benjamin Franklin invented a glass harmonica.

THE FIRST ANIMALS LAUNCHED INTO OUTER SPACE?

FRUIT FLIES.

50

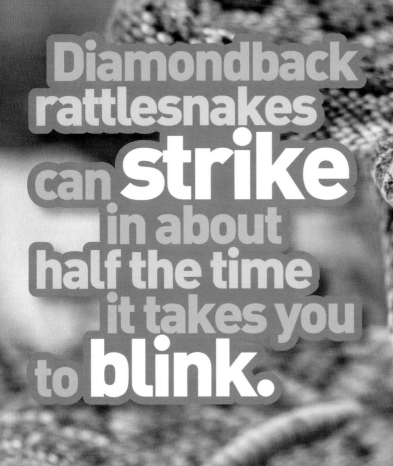

Diamondback rattlesnakes can **strike** in about half the time it takes you to **blink.**

An **artist** created the world's largest **biodegradable portrait** on a grassy slope in Switzerland.

Scientists recently discovered a glowing purple blob on the floor of the Pacific Ocean.

A FAST-FOOD RESTAURANT ONCE GAVE AWAY FRIED-CHICKEN-SCENTED SUNSCREEN.

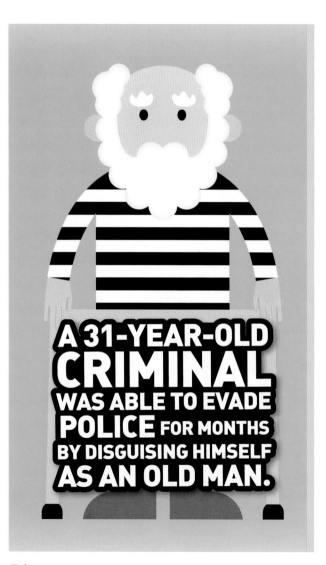

A 31-YEAR-OLD **CRIMINAL** WAS ABLE TO EVADE **POLICE** FOR MONTHS BY DISGUISING HIMSELF **AS AN OLD MAN.**

THE **U.S.** STATES OF ALASKA AND HAWAII HAVE THE SAME RECORD-HIGH TEMPERATURE: 100°F. (37.8°C)

AN **ARTIST** IN PHILADELPHIA, PENNSYLVANIA, U.S.A., CREATES **ART** USING DISCARDED CANDY WRAPPERS.

COCKROACHES ARE MORE LIKELY TO FLY IN HOT WEATHER.

THE PACIFIC BEETLE COCKROACH

58

Cockroaches have a built-in GPS!

HEY, GUYS, WAIT UP!

COCKROACH MILK IS MORE NUTRITIOUS THAN COW'S MILK.

PRODUCES MILK.

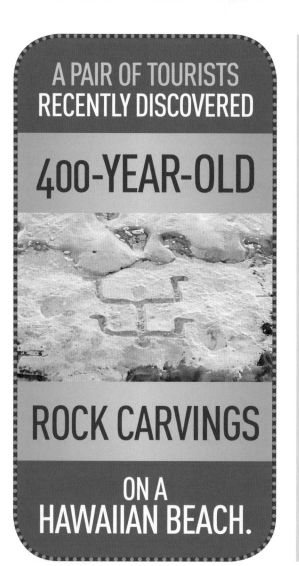

A PAIR OF TOURISTS RECENTLY DISCOVERED

400-YEAR-OLD

ROCK CARVINGS

ON A
HAWAIIAN BEACH.

It was once believed that massaging ground-up **pumpkin** onto your face could remove **freckles.**

A man in New York, U.S.A., returned a **library book** that was **15,531 days** (that's 42 years!) **overdue.**

DIVERS EXPLORING A SHIPWRECK OFF THE COAST OF SWEDEN FOUND A HUNK OF 340-YEAR-OLD CHEESE INSIDE A SEALED CONTAINER.

The oldest known **orca**—nicknamed "Granny"—lived to be 105.

Firefighting was an unofficial event at the 1900 Summer Olympics in Paris, France.

THE VIDEO GAME CHARACTER **MARIO** WAS ORIGINALLY NAMED **JUMPMAN.**

MINIATURE BLACK HOLES MAY BE

PASSING THROUGH EARTH EVERY DAY, A STUDY FOUND.

TEN PERCENT OF THE WORLD'S REDHEADS LIVE IN IRELAND.

Ireland is about the size of South Carolina, U.S.A.

A 1,075-year-old pine tree in Greece is the oldest known living thing in Europe.

SOME RATTLESNAKES IN THE GRAND CANYON ARE PINK.

A mouse scurrying through displays at the Museum of English Rural Life in Great Britain got caught in a 155-year-old mousetrap.

SEA STARS DON'T HAVE BLOOD.

Great frigate birds can fly for two months straight without landing.

THEY **NAP** WHILE THEY'RE FLYING.

SCIENTISTS
THINK THAT BOTH
REPTILES
AND BIRDS MAY
DREAM WHILE
SLEEPING.

THE EARTH'S SURFACE IS TWO AND A HALF YEARS OLDER THAN ITS CORE.

73

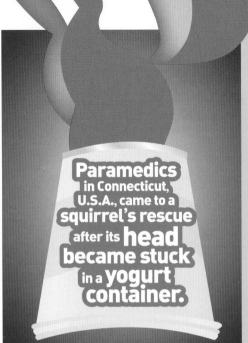

Paramedics in Connecticut, U.S.A., came to a **squirrel's rescue** after its **head became stuck** in a **yogurt container.**

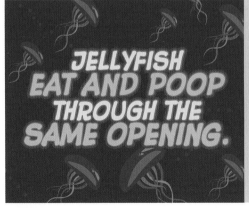

JELLYFISH EAT AND POOP THROUGH THE SAME OPENING.

A *bakery* in *London sells a* *doughnut* topped with caviar, gold leaf, gold vanilla beans, and a rare type of chocolate. *The price tag?* £1,500, or about $2,000.

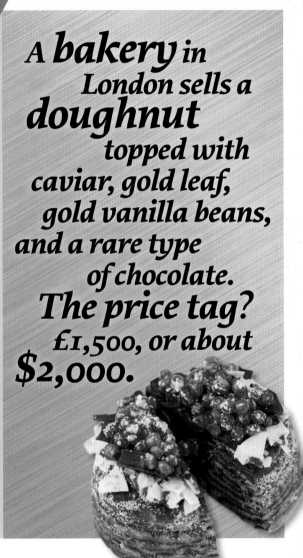

A friendly **stray dog** followed an **ultramarathon runner** for **77 miles** (124 km) in China's Gobi desert.

HOW'S MY PACE?

Chameleon **spit** is 400 times thicker than human spit.

SCIENTISTS USED A
3-D PRINTER TO MAKE
A PROSTHETIC BEAK
FOR A GOOSE MISSING MOST OF HER BILL.

A NEW YORK RESTAURANT
SERVES PIZZA
IN A BOX

MADE OF PIZZA.

When a **bee stings,**
it releases a chemical
that smells like
bananas.

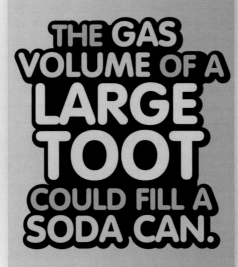

THE GAS VOLUME OF A LARGE TOOT COULD FILL A SODA CAN.

Underwater **volcanoes** cover more of the **Earth** than deserts or tundras.

THREE-TOED SLOTHS BURN ONLY 110 CALORIES A DAY— ABOUT THE SAME AS A HUMAN PLAYING SOCCER FOR 10 MINUTES.

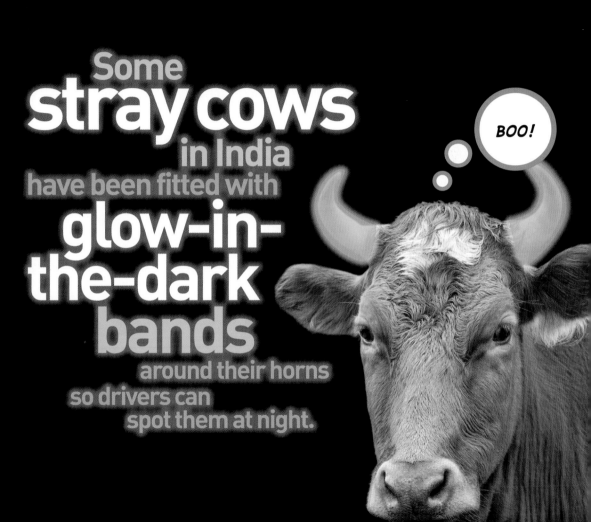

Some **stray cows** in India have been fitted with **glow-in-the-dark bands** around their horns so drivers can spot them at night.

BOO!

PARTS OF **BEIJING, CHINA,** ARE SINKING BY UP TO **FOUR** INCHES (10.2 cm) A YEAR, A STUDY SHOWED.

Most **kangaroos** are left-handed.

MILLIONS OF MOSQUITOES CAN FORM TWISTING, TORNADO-LIKE SWARMS THAT CAN REACH UP TO 1,000 (305 m) FEET TALL.

JANUARY 14 IS
DRESS UP
YOUR PET DAY.

NEVER FORCE YOUR
PET TO DO OR WEAR
ANYTHING IT
DOESN'T WANT TO.

SCIENTISTS TRAINED **HORSES** TO COMMUNICATE WITH PEOPLE USING SYMBOLS.

HORSE HOOVES NEVER STOP GROWING.

OOH, A WARM SPOT!

FISH **PEE** HELPS

CORAL REEFS THRIVE.

An **alligator** was seen using **a crosswalk** in northern Florida, U.S.A.

IS THERE A PROBLEM, OFFICER?

GUINEA PIGS OFTEN SLEEP WITH THEIR EYES OPEN.

PLAYING 3-D VIDEO GAMES CAN IMPROVE YOUR MEMORY, A STUDY FOUND.

DØDSING=
BELLY FLOPPING OFF
A THREE-STORY-TALL
PLATFORM

IT HAS SNOWED IN THE SAHARA.

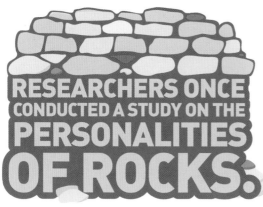

RESEARCHERS ONCE CONDUCTED A STUDY ON THE PERSONALITIES OF ROCKS.

Toads don't have teeth (but frogs do).

A mama moose gave birth to a calf in a shopping center parking lot in Anchorage, Alaska, U.S.A.

A **SIX-TON** (5.4-t) **"POTATO"** FLOATED ON A BARGE ALONG A RIVER IN NEW YORK, U.S.A.

www.bigidahopotato.com

A BIG HELPING

The Famous Idaho Potato Tour

YOU'LL KNOW **IT'S REAL** When You See the Seal!

DID SOMEONE SAY FRENCH FRIES?

A REAL POTATO THAT SIZE COULD MAKE 1.5 MILLION FRENCH FRIES.

You can go to elf school in Reykjavík, Iceland.

0.001 PERCENT OF YOUR **TAN** COMES FROM PHOTONS LEFT OVER FROM THE **BIG BANG.**

The Royal Norwegian Guard promoted a **penguin** named Sir Nils Olav III to **brigadier,** one of its **highest honors.**

Invisible poems
were painted on
sidewalks
in Boston, Massachusetts, U.S.A.

MY NOTES THE W

SNOW H

LOOKS LIKE BETWEEN 'EM THEY DONE

TRIED TO MAKE ME

STOP LAUGHIN' STOP LOVIN' STOP LIVIN'

BUT I DON'T CARE!

I'M STILL HERE!

N HU

YOU CAN SEE THEM ONLY WHEN THE GROUND GETS WET.

The Eiffel Tower seems smaller if you lean left while looking at it.

FARMERS IN SUNDERLAND, MASSACHUSETTS, U.S.A., DESIGNED A **CORN MAZE** INSPIRED BY THE NOVEL *ALICE'S ADVENTURES IN WONDERLAND.*

TEETH
CAN GROW ANYWHERE THROUGHOUT THE BODY— INCLUDING INSIDE YOUR
NOSE.

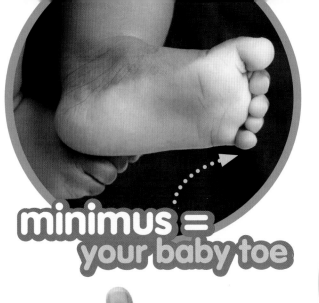

minimus =
your baby toe

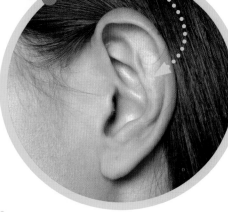

pinna =
the outer part
of your ear

purlicue =
the space between
your thumb and
forefinger

SOME SPECIES OF **MICROBES** IN YOUR GUT HAVE BEEN EVOLVING **FOR MILLIONS OF YEARS.**

oops!

A MONKEY TRIGGERED A **NATIONWIDE BLACKOUT** AFTER TRIPPING A TRANSFORMER ON THE ROOF OF A POWER PLANT IN KENYA.

A ranch in Texas, U.S.A., is two-thirds the size of Rhode Island.

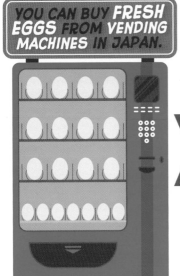

YOU CAN BUY **FRESH EGGS** FROM VENDING MACHINES IN JAPAN.

A **DOG** NAMED **DUKE** IS THE **MAYOR OF CORMORANT, MINNESOTA, U.S.A.**

Scientists use **rainbows** to study air pollution.

One hundred years ago, New York City **taxi cabs** were painted green and red, not **yellow**.

SWEET TREATS MAKE BEES FEEL OPTIMISTIC, ONE STUDY FOUND.

A MAN DRESSED AS **DARTH VADER** WAS SPOTTED PICKING UP **TRASH** ALONGSIDE A **HIGHWAY** IN VIRGINIA, U.S.A.

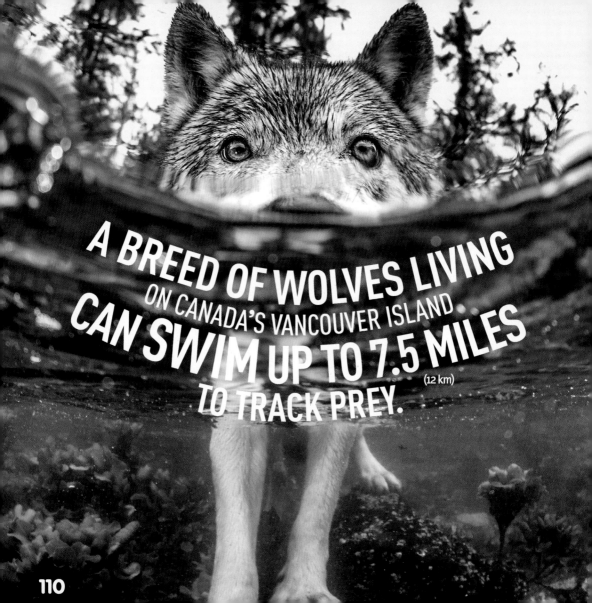

A BREED OF WOLVES LIVING ON CANADA'S VANCOUVER ISLAND CAN SWIM UP TO 7.5 MILES (12 km) TO TRACK PREY.

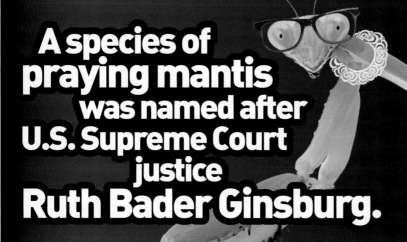

A species of praying mantis was named after U.S. Supreme Court justice Ruth Bader Ginsburg.

A popular fast-food restaurant in India sells chicken inside a container that can charge your cell phone.

FRUIT FLIES CAN SUFFER FROM INSOMNIA.

Yawning
may help
cool
your brain.

ANIMALS WITH **LARGE** BRAINS YAWN LONGER THAN ANIMALS WITH **SMALL** BRAINS.

A **BEAR** IN NEW MEXICO, U.S.A., **HITCHED A RIDE** ON TOP OF A **GARBAGE TRUCK** FOR **FIVE MILES** BEFORE CLIMBING OFF.

(8 km)

During the **world's longest race**, runners cover almost **60 miles** (97 km) **a day for 52 days.**

A small swimming snail known as a **sea butterfly** flaps its tiny wings to move through the water.

snotbot:
A ROBOT THAT COLLECTS WHALE SNOT FOR STUDY

A BLUE HOLE NEARLY AS DEEP AS THE HEIGHT OF THE EMPIRE STATE BUILDING WAS RECENTLY DISCOVERED IN THE SOUTH CHINA SEA.

MOST ANIMALS DON'T CHEW THEIR FOOD.

SCOTLAND'S **NATIONAL** ANIMAL IS A **UNICORN.**

According to researchers in Australia, **eating bananas** can make **human toots** less smelly.

petrichor = the smell in the air following rain

DON'T TRY THIS AT HOME!

One **summer**, residents of **Philadelphia**, Pennsylvania, U.S.A., swam in **Dumpster** "**pools**" to beat the heat.

121

CHICKENS ARE GENETICALLY CLOSER TO DINOSAURS THAN THEY ARE TO OTHER BIRDS.

Pacu fish crack open seeds and nuts with their humanlike teeth.

SEABIRD POOP *HELPS KEEP THE ARCTIC CLIMATE* **COOL.**

Tossing a **ball** of **aluminum foil** in your dryer can fight **static electricity.**

A *suit of armor* *for a* **guinea pig**— *complete with a jacket and tiny helmet*— *sold online for more than* **$24,000.**

A SINGLE **LAKE** IN SIBERIA CONTAINS **ONE-FIFTH** OF ALL **THE FRESHWATER** IN THE WORLD.

A giraffe can clean its nose with its tongue.

THE LONGEST-LASTING LIGHTNING BOLT EVER RECORDED WAS 7.74 SECONDS.

SPIDERS HEAR WITH THEIR LEGS.

A chef in New York City created a **doughnut** made from **purple yams** and dipped in **edible gold.**

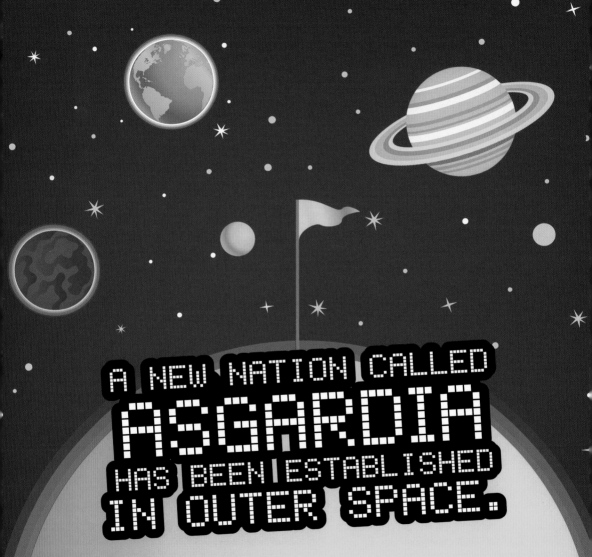

A NEW NATION CALLED **ASGARDIA** HAS BEEN ESTABLISHED IN OUTER SPACE.

RESEARCHERS RECENTLY FOUND INTACT **2,000-YEAR-OLD HUMAN REMAINS** ON A SHIPWRECK OFF THE COAST OF GREECE.

AT BIRTH, A GIANT PACIFIC OCTOPUS IS ABOUT THE SIZE OF A MOSQUITO.

The smallest mammal ever—**a prehistoric rodent**—was as big as your fingernail and weighed no more than a dollar bill.

Baby jackals eat their parents' vomit.

THE **FOREST CANOPY** IN THE **AMAZON** IS SO THICK THAT IT CAN TAKE **10 MINUTES** FOR RAIN TO REACH FROM THE TOP OF THE TREES TO **THE GROUND.**

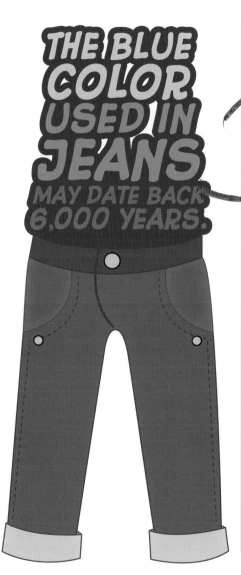

THE BLUE COLOR USED IN JEANS MAY DATE BACK 6,000 YEARS.

A WATER BUG NATIVE TO SOUTHEAST ASIA

CAN GROW AS BIG AS YOUR PALM.

A CHICKEN NAMED PATRICK PLAYS THE PIANO BY PECKING THE KEYS WITH HIS BEAK.

A HONEYBEE CAN LIFT ABOUT
80 PERCENT OF ITS
BODY WEIGHT IN POLLEN.

WHALES CAN TASTE ONLY SALTY FOODS.

Some
hermit
crabs
use discarded
trash as
shells.

Residents of Green Bank, West Virginia, U.S.A., can't use **Wi-Fi** because of a **high-tech** government **telescope** located there.

RADIOS AND CELL PHONES ARE ALSO **BANNED.**

TURTLES MAY HAVE FIRST EVOLVED SHELLS TO HELP THEM BURROW INTO THE EARTH.

Researchers have developed **edible** **packaging** for food.

99 PERCENT
OF MICROBE SPECIES
HAVE NOT YET BEEN DISCOVERED,
SCIENTISTS ESTIMATE.

THE SIZE OF A LARGE PIZZA, THE **COIN** WEIGHS **220 POUNDS.**

(100 kg)

CANADA HAS PRODUCED A MILLION-DOLLAR COIN.

City bees pollinate more plants than **country bees** do, a study found.

Pumpkins are 90 percent water.

IN SPAIN, THE TOOTH FAIRY IS A MOUSE NAMED PÉREZ.

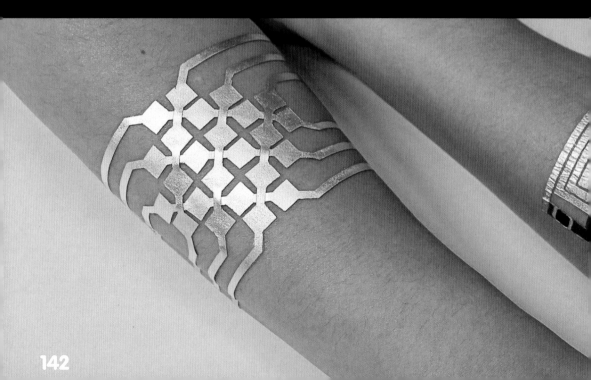

SCIENTISTS MADE TEMPORARY TATTOOS THAT CAN BE USED TO CONTROL SMARTPHONES.

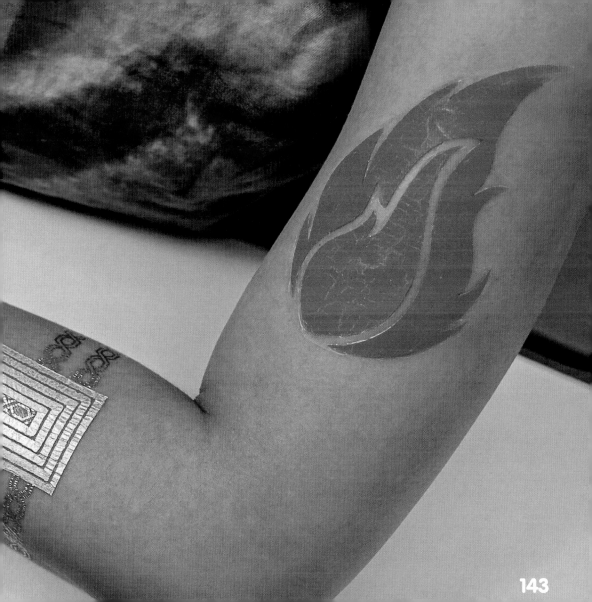

A **cat** once co-authored **a physics paper.**

SOME ANCIENT **MUMMIES** HAVE BEEN FOUND WITH MUMMIFIED HEAD LICE.

THERE IS AN **ASTEROID** SHAPED LIKE A **DOG BONE.**

Some trees know when their branches have been nibbled by an animal.

SCIENTISTS DISCOVERED A NEW SPIDER SPECIES THAT LOOKS LIKE A DRIED-UP LEAF.

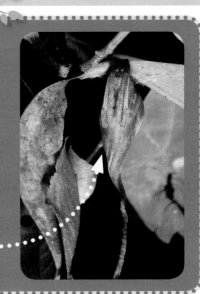

There's a huge heart-shaped ice patch on the surface of Pluto.

THAT'S WEIRD!

Baby hedgehogs are called hoglets.

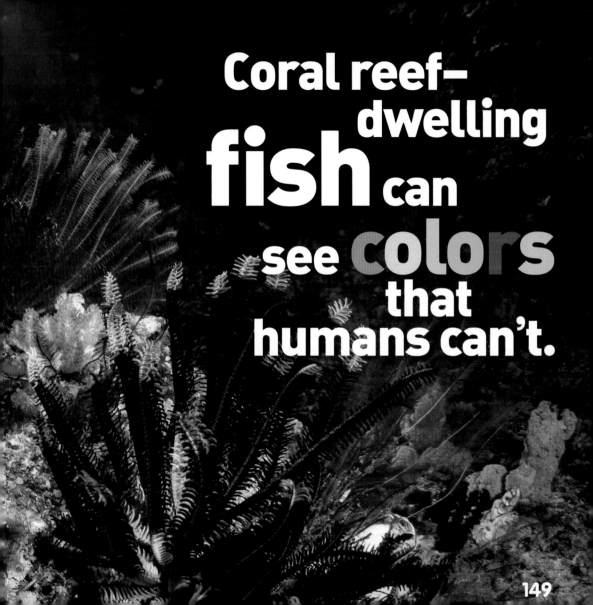

Coral reef–dwelling **fish** can see **colors** that humans can't.

Hot, dry weather caused piles of **horse poop** to **burst into flames** outside a **stable** in upstate New York, U.S.A.

THE POLICE HEADQUARTERS KNOWN AS **SCOTLAND YARD** IS NOT IN SCOTLAND.

Female donkeys are called **jennys.** Males are called **jacks.**

Scientists built an engine small enough to fit inside a **human cell.**

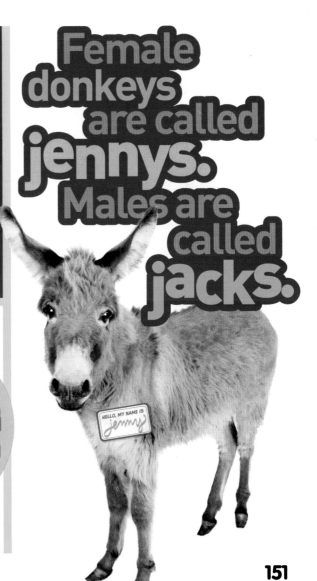

HELLO, MY NAME IS *Jenny*

U.S. PRESIDENT GEORGE WASHINGTON NEVER LIVED IN THE WHITE HOUSE.

IN BOTH 1841 AND 1881 THERE WERE THREE U.S. PRESIDENTS IN ONE YEAR.

THERE'S A FLOWER SHOP, A CHOCOLATE SHOP, AND A BOWLING ALLEY IN THE WHITE HOUSE BASEMENT.

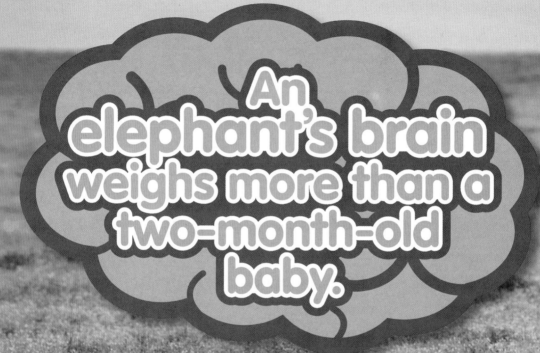

An elephant's brain weighs more than a two-month-old baby.

WATER BEETLES MAKE **HOMES** IN ELEPHANT FOOTPRINTS.

A pet dog named Keon **has a record-setting tail** that's as long as a **skateboard.**

Q is the only **letter of** the alphabet that does not appear in the **name** of any **U.S. state.**

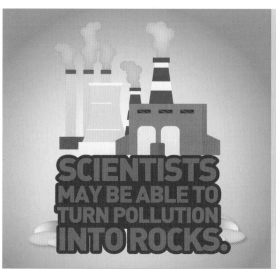

SCIENTISTS MAY BE ABLE TO TURN POLLUTION INTO ROCKS.

Some dinosaurs **quacked** like **ducks**, according to a recent study.

ONLY ONE SPECIES OF INSECT LIVES YEAR-ROUND IN ANTARCTICA.

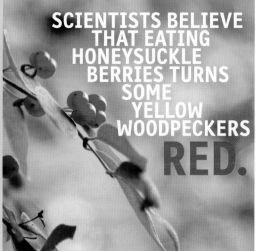

SCIENTISTS BELIEVE THAT EATING HONEYSUCKLE BERRIES TURNS SOME YELLOW WOODPECKERS RED.

A man in Florida, U.S.A., robbed a farmers market while wearing **a tutu.**

AT A CONTEST IN SLOVAKIA, **GRAVE DIGGERS** GO SHOVEL TO SHOVEL TO SEE WHO CAN DIG THE FASTEST— AND TIDIEST— **GRAVE.**

Catfish whiskers are known as **barbells.**

There's a **contest** to come up with the **worst sound** in the **world.**

Submissions included the sounds of **chili being stirred** and **nails** on a chalkboard.

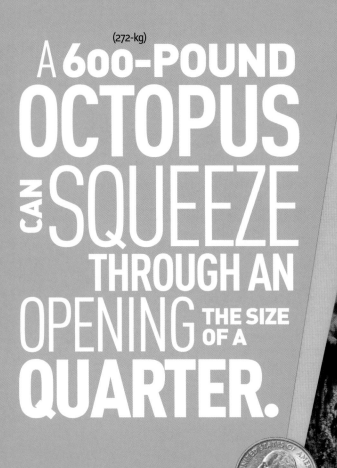

A **600-POUND** (272-kg) OCTOPUS CAN SQUEEZE THROUGH AN OPENING THE SIZE OF A QUARTER.

SCIENTISTS NICKNAMED A PATCH OF UNUSUALLY WARM PACIFIC OCEAN WATER "THE BLOB."

Cookie Monster said his name used to be Sid.

Scientists found a huge **lake** under a **volcano** in Bolivia.

SOME **BIRDS' BEAKS HAVE BUILT-IN AIR CONDITIONERS.**

A giant anteater flicks its tongue in and out of its mouth up to 150 times per minute.

HAPPY COWS MAKE MORE NUTRITIOUS MILK.

SOME SNAILS HIT PREDATORS WITH THEIR SHELLS.

SOME SCORPIONS HAVE 12 EYES.

An **ice-cream shop** in England is testing using a **drone** to deliver its **treats** to customers.

Nine-banded **armadillos** almost always give birth to **identical quadruplets.**

Scientists recently discovered a **jellyfish** that looks like a **glowing UFO.**

HUNDREDS OF STRAY CATS
ROAM AROUND DISNEYLAND, IN
CALIFORNIA, U.S.A., AT NIGHT
TO CATCH **REAL-LIFE MICE.**

A large green **snake** stowed away on **a plane** **flying** to Mexico City.

A **TEEN** IN WASHINGTON STATE, U.S.A., ONCE GOT HER **HEAD** STUCK INSIDE A GIANT **PUMPKIN.**

DON'T TRY THIS AT HOME!

THE **SKIN** OF ONE KIND OF SMALL AMAZONIAN **FROG** IS COVERED WITH **ANT** REPELLENT.

PLANTS MAY GROW FASTER IF YOU PLAY MUSIC FOR THEM.

171

YOU CAN **EAT** A MEAL IN AN **AIRPLANE-THEMED** RESTAURANT— **INSIDE** AN ACTUAL **PLANE**— IN WUHAN, CHINA.

THE FIRST WOMAN
TO RUN FOR
U.S. PRESIDENT
RAN BEFORE
WOMEN COULD
VOTE.

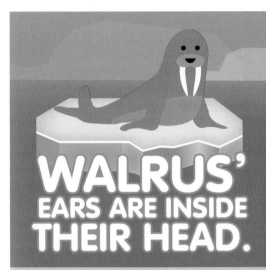

WALRUS' EARS ARE INSIDE THEIR HEAD.

Fireflies in the western United States don't glow.

AN INDIANA, U.S.A., COMPANY DESIGNED **PORTABLE TOILETS** THAT LIGHT UP AND SING **CHRISTMAS CAROLS.**

#JINGLEJOHNS

#JINGLEJOHNS
Service
Sanitation

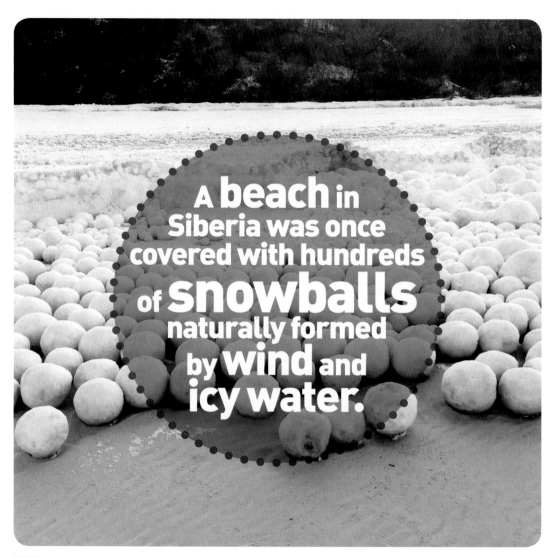

A **beach** in Siberia was once covered with hundreds of **snowballs** naturally formed by **wind** and **icy water.**

Civil War–era **cannonballs** washed up on a South Carolina, U.S.A., **beach** after a hurricane.

IT COULD TAKE **300 years** TO DISCOVER EVERY SPECIES OF **tree** IN THE Amazon rain forest.

Some birds use "**baby talk**" when singing to chicks.

goo-goo ga-ga

A couple tied the knot during a roller coaster ride in North Carolina, U.S.A.

Each year, Americans throw away some $60 million in loose change.

Only 8 percent of U.S. money is paper and coins (the rest is just numbers on a computer).

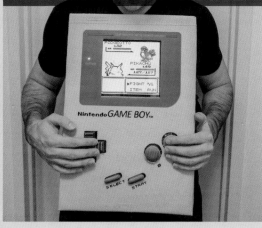

A NEW YORK MAN CREATED A VIDEO-GAME-THEMED HALLOWEEN COSTUME THAT PLAYS AN ACTUAL VIDEO GAME.

A HUNTSMAN SPIDER CAN GROW AS BIG AS A DINNER PLATE.

GORILLAS CAN CATCH HUMAN COLDS.

FISH CALLED SKATES CAN SEE ONLY IN BLACK AND WHITE.

U.S. PRESIDENT BARACK OBAMA ONCE WORKED AT AN ICE-CREAM SHOP.

YOU CAN ORDER SCOOPS OF PEAR-AND-BLUE-CHEESE-FLAVORED ICE CREAM AT A SHOP IN PORTLAND, OREGON, U.S.A.

ASPARAGUS, OYSTER, AND PARMESAN CHEESE WERE POPULAR ICE-CREAM FLAVORS IN THE UNITED STATES IN THE 18TH CENTURY.

An Italian man piled **121 scoops** of ice cream onto one cone.

A **hotel** in the Grand Canyon Caverns is 220 feet underground.

(67 m)

Northern stargazer fish zap their predators with a jolt of electricity.

Road **noise** from nearby **highways** can make it hard for some animals to **sniff out** predators.

A FOSSIL HUNTER IN THE U.K. FOUND A "**PICKLED**" DINOSAUR BRAIN.

THOUSANDS OF YEARS AGO, SOME PEOPLE CARRIED WATER AROUND IN HOLLOWED **OSTRICH EGGS.**

MICE CAN FEEL EACH **other's pain.**

A FLOCK OF **FLYING** **WiLD** TURKEYS CAUSED POWER OUTAGES IN AN OREGON, U.S.A., TOWN.

DUNG BEETLES TAKE MENTAL "SNAPSHOTS" OF THE NIGHT SKY.

wheee!

Dogs in the U.K. were trained to **fly** an **airplane.**

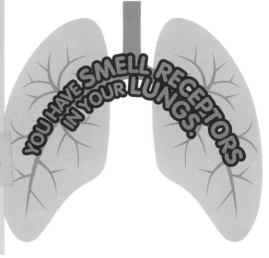

Warty Goblin, Cinderella, and **Wee-B-Little** are all types of **pumpkins.**

YOU HAVE SMELL RECEPTORS IN YOUR LUNGS.

SOME
DINOSAURS
HAD FOREST-
CAMOUFLAGE
COLORING.

THE FIRST MODERN COMPUTER WEIGHED 30 TONS.
(27 t)

THAT'S HEAVY!

THE FIRST CELL PHONE, NICKNAMED "THE BRICK," WEIGHED TWO POUNDS. (0.9 kg)

RESEARCHERS FOUND THAT RATS THAT LISTENED TO MOZART LEARNED TO RUN MAZES FASTER THAN RATS THAT LISTENED TO OTHER MUSIC.

SOME FROG CALLS CAN BE HEARD UP TO A MILE AWAY.

(1.6 km)

A baby echidna is called a puggle.

TREES "SLEEP" AT NIGHT.

Tadpoles eat **vegetarian meals** during heat waves.

RESEARCHERS HAVE FOUND A WAY TO **USE** SEWAGE TO **MAKE** FUEL.

Dog fleas jump higher than cat fleas.

U.S. TOWNS AND CITIES WITH THE

Good Grief, Idaho

Plenty Bears, South Dakota

Zzzyzx, California

Ding Dong, Texas

STRANGEST NAMES INCLUDE...

Goobertown, Arkansas

Lizard Lick, North Carolina

Boar Tush, Alabama

NORTH CAROLINA

ARKANSAS

ALABAMA

FACTFINDER

Boldface indicates illustrations.

FACTFINDER

FACTFINDER

For more information, visit nationalgeographic.com, call 1-800-647-5463, or write to the following address:

National Geographic Partners
1145 17th Street N.W.
Washington, D.C. 20036-4688 U.S.A.

Visit us online at nationalgeographic.com/books

For librarians and teachers: ngchildrensbooks.org

More for kids from National Geographic: kids.nationalgeographic.com

For information about special discounts for bulk purchases, please contact National Geographic Books Special Sales: specialsales@natgeo.com

For rights or permissions inquiries, please contact National Geographic Books Subsidiary Rights: bookrights@natgeo.com

Designed by Rachael Hamm Plett, Moduza Design

Trade paperback ISBN: 978-1-4263-2893-0
Reinforced library binding ISBN: 978-1-4263-2894-7

Printed in China
17/PPS/1

The publisher would like to thank Jen Agresta, project editor; Avery Hurt, researcher and author; and Sarah Wassner Flynn, researcher and author.

Now YOU can be WEIRD 365 days a year!

This awesome daily planner is packed with fun facts, cool graphics, and plenty of space to write, doodle, and track assignments, activities, and get-togethers all year long.

NORWAY ONCE **KNIGHTED** A **PENGUIN** NAMED **SIR NILS OLAV.**

REPORTING FOR DUTY!

If you could name a penguin, what would you call it?

JANUARY 1

NEW YEAR'S DAY
MON | TUES | WED | THURS | FRI | SAT | SUN

2
MON | TUES | WED | THURS | FRI | SAT | SUN

MY GOALS FOR THIS MONTH

NATIONAL GEOGRAPHIC KIDS

weird but true!

DAILY PLANNER
365 Days to Fill with School, Sports, Friends, and Fun!